K. CONNORS

Java Programming for Beginners

Learn to Code, Master Java, and Build Real-World Applications

First edition

This book was professionally typeset on Reedsy.
Find out more at reedsy.com

Contents

Introduction: Getting Started with Java   1

Chapter 1: Introduction to Programming and Java   4

Chapter 2: Setting Up Your Java Environment   9

Chapter 3: Java Basics - Syntax, Variables, and Data Types   15

Chapter 4: Control Flow - Conditionals and Loops   23

Chapter 5: Functions and Methods   33

Chapter 6: Object-Oriented Programming (OOP) Concepts   40

Chapter 7: Working with Arrays and Collections   49

Chapter 8: Exception Handling   59

Chapter 9: Working with Files and I/O   69

Chapter 10: Basic Java APIs and Libraries   84

Conclusion: Your Journey in Java Programming   98

Introduction: Getting Started with Java

Welcome to the wonderful world of Java programming! If you've picked up this book, you're likely embarking on an exciting journey to learn one of the most popular and powerful programming languages out there. Whether you're a complete newbie or someone with a bit of coding experience looking to expand your skills, you're in the right place. Java is like the Swiss Army knife of programming languages – versatile, reliable, and equipped to handle just about anything you throw at it.

But before we dive into the nitty-gritty of code, let's take a moment to appreciate why Java is such a big deal. Java was born in the mid-90s, a time when the internet was still in its infancy and people were just starting to realize the potential of this new digital frontier. The folks at Sun Microsystems (the creators of Java) envisioned a language that was robust, secure, and platform-independent – meaning it could run on any device, whether it was a bulky desktop computer or a snazzy new mobile phone. Fast forward to today, and Java is everywhere: in web applications, mobile apps, enterprise software, and even in the embedded systems that power your home appliances.

So, what makes Java so special? For starters, it's an object-oriented programming (OOP) language. If that term sounds intimidating, don't worry – we'll break it down in a later chapter. For now, just think of OOP as a way of organizing your code into neat, reusable chunks. This makes your programs easier to manage, understand, and extend. Another great thing about Java is its syntax. Sure, it might look like gibberish at first glance, but once you get the hang of it, you'll find that Java's syntax is logical, consistent, and relatively easy to read.

One of the biggest reasons Java has stood the test of time is its motto: "Write once, run anywhere." Thanks to the Java Virtual Machine (JVM), you can write your Java code on one machine, and run it on virtually any other machine without having to worry about compatibility issues. This cross-platform capability is a huge advantage, especially in today's world where we use a multitude of devices.

Now, I know what you might be thinking: "This all sounds great, but can I really learn Java?" Absolutely! Learning Java is like learning a new language (literally), and just like picking up Spanish or French, it takes time, practice, and a bit of patience. But here's the good news: if you follow along with this book, take the time to try out the examples, and do the exercises, you'll be well on your way to becoming a competent Java programmer. And who knows? You might even have some fun along the way.

Let's talk about why you might want to learn Java in the first place. Perhaps you're interested in a career in software development. If so, Java is a fantastic choice. It's a language that's in high demand, with plenty of job opportunities. Companies from small startups to massive enterprises rely on Java for their backend systems, making it a valuable skill in the job market. Or maybe you're looking to build your own projects – whether it's a mobile app, a game, or even a tool to automate some boring tasks on your computer. Java's versatility and rich ecosystem of libraries and frameworks make it an excellent choice for all sorts of projects.

Learning Java also opens up a world of community and resources. Java has been around for over two decades, and in that time, a massive community of developers has grown around it. This means that no matter what problem you encounter, chances are someone else has faced it before and there's a solution out there. From forums and blogs to tutorials and courses, the wealth of resources available for Java is staggering.

But let's not get ahead of ourselves. Before we can build the next great app or land that dream job, we need to start with the basics. This book is designed to take you from ground zero to a place where you feel confident writing and understanding Java code. We'll start with setting up your programming environment – because, let's face it, nothing kills the excitement of learning like spending hours wrestling with installations. Once we've got everything up and running, we'll dive into the fundamental concepts of Java, gradually building up your knowledge and skills through practical examples and exercises.

Throughout this book, we'll also explore real-life scenarios where Java is used. This isn't just to make the material more interesting (though that's part of it), but to show you how the concepts we're learning apply in the real world. For example, when we talk about control flow, we might look at how an e-commerce website processes an order. When we discuss object-oriented programming, we'll see how these principles are used in building complex applications like video games or enterprise software.

By the end of this book, you won't just have a theoretical understanding of Java – you'll have practical skills that you can apply to your own projects. And who knows? You might even be inspired to dig deeper into more advanced topics, join a coding community, or start contributing to open-source projects.

So, grab a cup of coffee (or tea, if you prefer), get comfortable, and let's get started on this Java adventure. Remember, every expert was once a beginner. With a bit of curiosity, perseverance, and a willingness to experiment, you'll be amazed at what you can achieve. Welcome to Java programming for beginners – let's make some magic happen!

Chapter 1: Introduction to Programming and Java

Welcome to the first chapter of your journey into Java programming! We're going to dive into the basics of programming and how Java fits into this vast and exciting world. Think of this chapter as the first day of school – you're getting your bearings, meeting new concepts, and setting the foundation for everything that comes next.

Let's start with the basics: what exactly is programming? In simple terms, programming is the process of creating a set of instructions that tell a computer how to perform a task. These instructions are written in a language that the computer can understand and execute. Now, there are many programming languages out there – each with its own quirks, strengths, and ideal uses. Java is one of these languages, and it's a pretty special one at that.

Java was created in the mid-1990s by a team of developers at Sun Microsystems. They wanted to design a language that was simple, robust, and capable of running on any device, regardless of its hardware or operating system. The result was Java, a language that has become incredibly popular in the world of software development. Today, Java is used for everything from web applications and mobile apps to enterprise systems and embedded devices.

So, why did the creators of Java think the world needed yet another programming language? Well, at the time, most programming languages were either too specific to certain platforms (like C and C++), or they weren't robust enough to handle the demands of modern computing. Java was designed to be platform independent, meaning you could write your code once and run it anywhere. This concept is known as "Write Once, Run Anywhere" (WORA), and it's one of Java's most powerful features.

To understand how Java achieves this platform independence, we need to talk about the Java Virtual Machine (JVM). When you write a Java program, you're actually writing code that is compiled into an intermediate form called bytecode. This bytecode is then executed by the JVM, which is a piece of software that interprets the bytecode and runs it on your computer. The JVM is available for many different platforms, so as long as there's a JVM for your device, you can run Java code on it. Pretty cool, right?

Now that we've covered the high-level overview, let's get into some of the nitty-gritty details of Java itself. One of the first things you'll notice about Java is its syntax. Syntax refers to the rules and structure of the language – in other words, how you write your code. Java's syntax is similar to other programming languages like C and C++, which makes it relatively easy to learn if you have experience with those languages. But even if you're completely new to programming, don't worry – we'll take it step by step.

A basic Java program looks something like this:

```
public class HelloWorld {
    public static void main(String[] args) {
    System.out.println("Hello, World!");
    }
    }
```

Let's break this down. The first line, 'public class HelloWorld', is defining a class. In Java, everything is part of a class. Think of a class as a blueprint for

5

creating objects – it defines the properties and behaviors that the objects will have. In this case, our class is called 'HelloWorld'.

The next line, 'public static void main(String[] args)', is defining a method. A method is a block of code that performs a specific task. The 'main' method is special because it's the entry point of any Java program – it's where the program starts executing. The keywords 'public', 'static', and 'void' have specific meanings in Java, but for now, just know that they're necessary for defining the 'main' method.

Inside the 'main' method, we have a single line of code: 'System.out.println("Hello, World!");'. This line prints the text "Hello, World!" to the console. 'System.out' is an object that represents the standard output stream (i.e., your screen), and 'println' is a method that prints a line of text to that stream. The text inside the quotation marks is called a string, which is a sequence of characters.

Congratulations! You've just written and understood your first Java program. It might seem simple, but this "Hello, World!" example is a rite of passage for new programmers. It introduces you to the basic structure of a Java program and shows you how to produce output.

Before we move on, let's talk a bit about the development tools you'll need to write Java programs. First and foremost, you'll need the Java Development Kit (JDK). The JDK is a software development kit that includes everything you need to develop Java applications – the Java compiler, the JVM, and various other tools. You can download the JDK from Oracle's website, and it's available for all major operating systems.

Once you have the JDK installed, you'll also want an Integrated Development Environment (IDE). An IDE is a software application that provides a comprehensive environment for writing, testing, and debugging your code. There are many IDEs available for Java, but some of the most popular ones are IntelliJ

IDEA, Eclipse, and NetBeans. Each of these IDEs has its own set of features and advantages, so you might want to try a few and see which one you prefer.

With your tools in place, you're ready to start writing Java code. But where do you begin? One of the best ways to learn programming is by doing, so in this book, we'll be working through lots of examples and exercises. Each chapter will introduce new concepts and techniques, building on what you've learned previously. By the end of the book, you'll have a solid understanding of Java and be well-equipped to tackle your own projects.

To keep things interesting, we'll also explore real-life scenarios where Java is used. For example, we'll look at how Java powers web applications, mobile apps, and enterprise systems. These examples will help you see the practical applications of what you're learning and give you a sense of the many possibilities that Java programming opens up.

In addition to the technical details, we'll also cover some of the soft skills that are important for programmers. This includes things like debugging techniques, best practices for writing clean and maintainable code, and how to approach problem-solving. These skills are just as important as knowing the syntax of the language, and they'll serve you well throughout your programming career.

One of the key takeaways from this chapter is the importance of practice and experimentation. Programming is as much an art as it is a science, and the best way to learn is by doing. Don't be afraid to make mistakes – they're a natural part of the learning process. Try out the examples, modify them, and see what happens. The more you play around with code, the more comfortable you'll become.

Another important point is to stay curious and keep learning. The world of programming is constantly evolving, with new languages, frameworks, and tools emerging all the time. Java itself has gone through many changes since its inception, and staying up-to-date with the latest developments will help you stay relevant in the field.

Finally, remember that you're not alone on this journey. The programming community is vast and welcoming, with countless resources available to help you. From online forums and tutorials to local coding meetups and conferences, there are many ways to connect with other programmers and share your experiences.

So, as we wrap up this first chapter, take a moment to reflect on why you're learning Java and what you hope to achieve. Whether you're aiming for a new career, looking to build your own projects, or simply satisfying your curiosity, you're taking a significant step forward. Embrace the challenges, celebrate the victories, and enjoy the journey.

Welcome to the world of Java programming – let's get coding!

Chapter 2: Setting Up Your Java Environment

Alright, now that we've dipped our toes into the world of Java programming, it's time to get our hands dirty with setting up your Java environment. Think of this chapter as prepping your kitchen before you start cooking a gourmet meal. You wouldn't want to start without making sure you have all the ingredients and tools ready, right? The same goes for programming. Let's make sure we have everything we need to start writing and running Java code.

Downloading and Installing the JDK

First things first, you'll need the Java Development Kit (JDK). This is like your all-in-one toolbox that contains the compiler, libraries, and other utilities you'll need to write Java programs. The JDK is available for free from Oracle, and you can download it from their website. But before you do that, let's figure out which version of the JDK you need.

Java has gone through many versions over the years, and it can be a bit overwhelming to decide which one to choose. As a beginner, it's best to start with the latest Long-Term Support (LTS) version, which at the time of writing is Java 17. LTS versions are supported for a longer period, ensuring stability and security updates, which makes them a safe bet for beginners.

Installing the JDK

Head over to the Oracle website and look for the JDK download page. You'll see options for different operating systems – Windows, macOS, and Linux. Choose the one that matches your operating system, download the installer, and follow the prompts to install it. Once the installation is complete, you'll need to set up your system's environment variables so your computer knows where to find the Java tools.

Setting Up Environment Variables on Windows

If you're on Windows, open the Start menu, type "Environment Variables," and select the option to edit them. Click on the "New" button to create a new system variable named JAVA_HOME and set its value to the path where you installed the JDK (something like C:\Program Files\Java\jdk-17). Next, find the "Path" variable in the list, edit it, and add a new entry pointing to the bin directory inside your JDK installation path. This tells your system where to find the Java compiler and other tools.

Setting Up Environment Variables on macOS and Linux

On macOS and Linux, you'll need to edit your shell's profile file. Open a terminal and type nano ~/.bash_profile (or ~/.zshrc if you're using the Zsh shell). Add the following lines at the end of the file:

export   JAVA_HOME=/Library/Java/JavaVirtualMachines/jdk-17.jdk/Contents/Home
   export PATH=$JAVA_HOME/bin:$PATH

Save the file and run source ~/.bash_profile to apply the changes. You can verify your setup by opening a new terminal and typing java -version. If everything is set up correctly, you should see the version of Java you installed.

Choosing an IDE

Now that we have the JDK installed, let's talk about Integrated Development Environments (IDEs). An IDE is a software application that provides comprehensive facilities to computer programmers for software development. This typically includes a source code editor, build automation tools, and a debugger. For Java, some of the most popular IDEs are IntelliJ IDEA, Eclipse, and NetBeans.

Setting Up IntelliJ IDEA

Let's start with IntelliJ IDEA. Developed by JetBrains, IntelliJ IDEA is known for its powerful features, intelligent code assistance, and user-friendly interface. It comes in two versions: a free Community edition and a paid Ultimate edition. The Community edition is more than enough for beginners, so go ahead and download it from the JetBrains website. Once downloaded, run the installer and follow the prompts to set it up.

When you first open IntelliJ IDEA, you'll be greeted with a welcome screen. Click on "New Project" and select "Java" from the list of project types. You'll be asked to specify the JDK location − IntelliJ should automatically detect the JDK you installed earlier, but if it doesn't, you can browse to the installation directory manually. Click "Next" a few times, and you'll have a new Java project ready to go.

Setting Up Eclipse

Eclipse is another popular IDE for Java development. It's open-source and has a huge community of users and contributors. You can download Eclipse from their official website. The installation process is straightforward − download the installer, run it, and select "Eclipse IDE for Java Developers." Once installed, open Eclipse and create a new Java project by selecting "File" -> "New" -> "Java Project." Name your project and click "Finish."

Setting Up NetBeans

NetBeans, another powerful IDE, is also a great choice for beginners. It's sponsored by Apache and offers robust support for Java, along with many other languages. Download NetBeans from the official website, run the installer, and follow the prompts. After installation, open NetBeans and create a new project by going to "File" -> "New Project" -> "Java" -> "Java Application."

Writing Your First Java Program

With your IDE set up, let's write our first Java program. Open your IDE and create a new Java file in your project. Name it HelloWorld.java and type the following code:

```java
public class HelloWorld {
    public static void main(String[] args) {
    System.out.println("Hello, World!");
    }
    }
```

This is a simple program that prints "Hello, World!" to the console. To run it, right-click on the file and select "Run" (or click the play button in IntelliJ IDEA). If everything is set up correctly, you should see the output in the console at the bottom of the IDE. Congratulations, you've just written and executed your first Java program!

Using a Text Editor and Command Line

At this point, you might be thinking, "This is great, but why do I need an IDE? Can't I just write my code in a text editor and run it from the command line?" You absolutely can, and in fact, it's a good idea to understand how to do that. Let's give it a try.

Open a text editor (Notepad on Windows, TextEdit on macOS, or nano on Linux) and type the same HelloWorld program as before. Save the file as HelloWorld.java in a directory of your choice. Now, open a terminal or command prompt, navigate to the directory where you saved the file, and type the following commands:

```
javac HelloWorld.java
  java HelloWorld
```

The javac command compiles your Java file into bytecode, creating a HelloWorld.class file. The java command runs the compiled bytecode using the JVM. If everything goes well, you should see "Hello, World!" printed to the console.

The Advantages of Using an IDE

Using a text editor and the command line to write and run Java programs is a great way to understand the basics of how Java works. However, as your programs become more complex, you'll appreciate the features that an IDE provides, such as code completion, debugging tools, and project management.

Importance of Setting Up Your Environment

One of the best things about setting up your Java environment is that it's a one-time effort. Once everything is in place, you can focus on writing code and learning new concepts without worrying about configuration issues. Plus, getting comfortable with your development tools is an important part of becoming a proficient programmer.

Continuing Your Java Journey

As you continue your journey into Java programming, remember that setting up your environment is just the beginning. The real fun starts when you begin writing code, experimenting with different concepts, and building your own projects. Don't be afraid to explore and try out different tools and techniques – the more you practice, the better you'll become.

Summary

In summary, setting up your Java environment involves downloading and installing the JDK, configuring your system's environment variables, and choosing an IDE that suits your needs. Whether you go with IntelliJ IDEA, Eclipse, NetBeans, or stick with a text editor and the command line, you're now equipped with the tools you need to start coding in Java. So, let's roll up our sleeves and get ready to dive into the world of Java programming. The adventure is just beginning!

Chapter 3: Java Basics - Syntax, Variables, and Data Types

Welcome to Chapter 3! Now that your Java environment is all set up and you've run your first "Hello, World!" program, it's time to dive deeper into the fundamentals of Java. Think of this chapter as learning the grammar and vocabulary of a new language. We'll cover the basic building blocks of Java: syntax, variables, and data types. By the end of this chapter, you'll have a solid foundation to build more complex programs.

Understanding Java Syntax

Let's start with syntax. Syntax in programming is like grammar in spoken languages. It defines the rules and structure for writing code that the Java compiler can understand. Java syntax might look intimidating at first, but once you get used to it, you'll find it's quite logical and consistent.

Every Java program is made up of classes and methods. Classes are the blueprints for objects, and methods are the actions that objects can perform. For example, in our "Hello, World!" program, 'HelloWorld' is a class, and 'main' is a method. The basic structure of a Java program looks something like this:

public class ClassName {

```
public static void main(String[] args) {
// code goes here
}
}
```

Here, 'public' is an access modifier that makes the class accessible from other classes. 'class' is a keyword used to define a class. 'ClassName' is the name of the class, and you can name it whatever you want, as long as it follows certain rules (it must start with a letter and can contain letters and numbers).

Inside the class, we have the 'main' method. The 'main' method is the entry point of any Java program. It's where the program starts executing. The line 'public static void main(String[] args)' might look like a mouthful, but it makes more sense once you break it down:
   - 'public' means the method can be called from anywhere.
   - 'static' means the method belongs to the class, not an instance of the class.
   - 'void' means the method doesn't return any value.
   - 'main' is the name of the method.
   - 'String[] args' is an array of 'String' objects that stores command-line arguments.

Declaring Variables

Next, let's talk about variables. Variables are used to store data that can be used and manipulated in your programs. Think of variables as containers that hold information. In Java, you need to declare a variable before you can use it. Declaring a variable involves specifying its data type and giving it a name. Here's the basic syntax for declaring a variable:

dataType variableName;

For example, to declare an integer variable named 'myNumber', you would write:

```
int myNumber;
```

You can also initialize a variable at the time of declaration by assigning it a value:

```
int myNumber = 10;
```

Java has several data types, and they can be broadly classified into two categories: primitive data types and reference data types. Let's start with primitive data types.

Primitive Data Types

Primitive data types are the most basic data types available in Java. They include:
- 'byte': 8-bit integer
- 'short': 16-bit integer
- 'int': 32-bit integer
- 'long': 64-bit integer
- 'float': 32-bit floating-point number
- 'double': 64-bit floating-point number
- 'char': 16-bit Unicode character
- 'boolean': true or false

Here's how you can declare and initialize variables of different primitive data types:

```
byte myByte = 100;
   short myShort = 10000;
   int myInt = 100000;
   long myLong = 100000L;
   float myFloat = 10.5f;
   double myDouble = 10.5;
```

```
char myChar = 'A';
boolean myBoolean = true;
```

Notice the 'L' at the end of the long value and the 'f' at the end of the float value. These suffixes are required to indicate that the values are of type long and float, respectively.

Reference Data Types

Reference data types, on the other hand, are used to refer to objects. They include classes, interfaces, and arrays. Unlike primitive data types, reference variables store addresses of objects in memory. For example, to declare a variable of type 'String', which is a class in Java, you would write:

```
String myString = "Hello, Java!";
```

Arrays

An array is a collection of variables of the same data type. It's like a list of items that are stored in contiguous memory locations. You can declare an array by specifying the data type followed by square brackets:

```
int[] myArray;
```

You can also initialize an array at the time of declaration by specifying the size of the array or by providing the elements directly:

```
int[] myArray = new int[5]; // an array of 5 integers
  int[] myArray = {1, 2, 3, 4, 5}; // an array with initial values
```

Accessing elements of an array is done using indices, with the first element at index 0:

```
int firstElement = myArray[0];
   int secondElement = myArray[1];
```

String Manipulation

Strings are sequences of characters and are one of the most commonly used data types in Java. The 'String' class provides many methods for manipulating strings, such as concatenation, comparison, and finding substrings. Here's an example of how you can work with strings:

```
String greeting = "Hello";
   String name = "World";
   String message = greeting + ", " + name + "!";
   System.out.println(message);
```

In this example, we concatenate (combine) the 'greeting' and 'name' variables to create a new string and print it to the console.

Type Casting

Sometimes, you might need to convert a variable from one data type to another. This process is called type casting. There are two types of type casting in Java: implicit (automatic) casting and explicit (manual) casting.

Implicit casting happens automatically when you assign a smaller data type to a larger data type:

```
int myInt = 10;
   double myDouble = myInt; // implicit casting
```

Explicit casting is required when you assign a larger data type to a smaller data type:

```java
double myDouble = 10.5;
    int myInt = (int) myDouble; // explicit casting
```

In this case, you need to specify the target data type in parentheses before the value.

Constants

If you want to declare a variable whose value should not change, you can use the 'final' keyword. Such variables are called constants:

```java
final int MY_CONSTANT = 100;
```

Once a constant is initialized, its value cannot be changed.

Operators

Operators are symbols that perform operations on variables and values. Java has several types of operators, including arithmetic, relational, logical, and assignment operators. Here are some examples:

Arithmetic operators: +, -, *, /, %
    Relational operators: ==, !=, >, <, >=, <=
    Logical operators: &&, ||, !
    Assignment operators: =, +=, -=, *=, /=, %=

Here's how you can use some of these operators in Java:

```java
int a = 10;
    int b = 5;
    int sum = a + b; // sum is 15
    boolean isEqual = (a == b); // isEqual is false
    boolean isGreater = (a > b); // isGreater is true
```

boolean result = (a > b) && (a != b); // result is true

Understanding and using these operators effectively is crucial for writing meaningful Java programs.

Takeaways

Alright, let's wrap up with some key takeaways from this chapter:
   - Java syntax defines the rules and structure for writing code that the Java compiler can understand.
   - Variables are used to store data and must be declared with a specific data type before use.
   - Primitive data types include byte, short, int, long, float, double, char, and boolean.
   - Reference data types include classes, interfaces, and arrays.
   - Arrays are collections of variables of the same data type, accessed using indices.
   - Strings are sequences of characters, and the String class provides many methods for manipulating them.
   - Type casting allows you to convert variables from one data type to another.
   - Constants are variables whose values cannot be changed and are declared using the final keyword.
   - Operators perform operations on variables and values, and understanding them is essential for writing effective Java programs.

By now, you should have a solid understanding of the basic building blocks of Java. These concepts might seem simple on the surface, but they're the foundation for everything you'll do in Java programming. So, keep practicing, experiment with different variables and operators, and try to build small programs using what you've learned.

With these basics under your belt, you're ready to move on to more advanced topics in Java programming. In the next chapter, we'll explore control flow in Java, including conditionals and loops. This will enable you to write more complex programs that can make decisions and repeat actions.

Chapter 4: Control Flow - Conditionals and Loops

Welcome to Chapter 4! Now that you're familiar with Java syntax, variables, and data types, it's time to introduce some decision-making abilities to your programs. Think of this chapter as teaching your Java code how to think for itself. We'll dive into control flow, which includes conditionals and loops. These concepts will allow your programs to make decisions and repeat actions, making them much more powerful and flexible.

Understanding Control Flow

In programming, control flow is the order in which individual statements, instructions, or function calls are executed or evaluated. In other words, control flow determines the path your program takes as it runs. Without control flow statements, your code would simply execute from top to bottom, which would be quite limiting. By using conditionals and loops, you can control the flow of your program and make it more dynamic and responsive.

Conditionals: if, else, and switch

Let's start with conditionals. Conditionals are statements that allow your program to execute certain code blocks based on whether a condition is true or false. The most common conditional statements in Java are if, else if, and else.

The if Statement

The if statement evaluates a condition (a boolean expression) and executes a block of code if the condition is true. Here's the basic syntax:

```
if (condition) {
    // code to be executed if condition is true
    }
```

For example, let's say you want to check if a number is positive:

```
int number = 10;
    if (number > 0) {
    System.out.println("The number is positive.");
    }
```

In this example, the condition (number > 0) is true, so the code inside the if block is executed, and the message "The number is positive." is printed to the console.

The else Statement

The else statement is used to execute a block of code if the condition in the if statement is false. Here's the syntax:

```
if (condition) {
    // code to be executed if condition is true
    } else {
    // code to be executed if condition is false
    }
```

For example, let's check if a number is positive or negative:

```
int number = -5;
   if (number > 0) {
   System.out.println("The number is positive.");
   } else {
   System.out.println("The number is negative.");
   }
```

In this case, the condition (number > 0) is false, so the code inside the else block is executed, and the message "The number is negative." is printed to the console.

The else if Statement

The else if statement is used to specify a new condition to test if the first condition is false. You can chain multiple else if statements to check multiple conditions. Here's the syntax:

```
if (condition1) {
   // code to be executed if condition1 is true
   } else if (condition2) {
   // code to be executed if condition2 is true
   } else {
   // code to be executed if all conditions are false
   }
```

For example, let's check if a number is positive, negative, or zero:

```
int number = 0;
   if (number > 0) {
   System.out.println("The number is positive.");
   } else if (number < 0) {
```

```
System.out.println("The number is negative.");
} else {
System.out.println("The number is zero.");
}
```

In this example, the first two conditions are false, so the code inside the else block is executed, and the message "The number is zero." is printed to the console.

The switch Statement

The switch statement is another way to control the flow of your program based on the value of a variable. It's particularly useful when you have multiple conditions to check, and it can make your code more readable than using multiple if-else statements. Here's the basic syntax:

```
switch (variable) {
    case value1:
    // code to be executed if variable equals value1
    break;
    case value2:
    // code to be executed if variable equals value2
    break;
    // more cases...
    default:
    // code to be executed if none of the cases match
    }
```

For example, let's use a switch statement to determine the day of the week based on an integer value:

```
int day = 3;
    switch (day) {
```

```java
case 1:
System.out.println("Sunday");
break;
case 2:
System.out.println("Monday");
break;
case 3:
System.out.println("Tuesday");
break;
case 4:
System.out.println("Wednesday");
break;
case 5:
System.out.println("Thursday");
break;
case 6:
System.out.println("Friday");
break;
case 7:
System.out.println("Saturday");
break;
default:
System.out.println("Invalid day");
break;
}
```

In this example, the variable 'day' equals 3, so the code inside the case 3 block is executed, and the message "Tuesday" is printed to the console.

Loops: for, while, and do-while

Loops are used to execute a block of code repeatedly based on a condition. They are incredibly useful for tasks that require repetition, such as iterating over arrays or processing user input. The most common loops in Java are for, while, and do-while.

The for Loop

The for loop is used to execute a block of code a specific number of times. It's often used when you know in advance how many times you want to repeat a task. Here's the basic syntax:

```
for (initialization; condition; update) {
   // code to be executed
   }
```

For example, let's print the numbers 1 to 5:

```
for (int i = 1; i <= 5; i++) {
   System.out.println(i);
   }
```

In this example, the initialization 'int i = 1' sets the starting value of 'i' to 1. The condition 'i <= 5' means the loop will continue as long as 'i' is less than or equal to 5. The update 'i++' increments the value of 'i' by 1 after each iteration.

The while Loop

The while loop is used to execute a block of code repeatedly as long as a condition is true. It's often used when you don't know in advance how many times you need to repeat a task. Here's the basic syntax:

```
while (condition) {
   // code to be executed
   }
```

For example, let's print the numbers 1 to 5 using a while loop:

```
int i = 1;
  while (i <- 5) {
  System.out.println(i);
  i++;
  }
```

In this example, the loop continues as long as the condition 'i <= 5' is true. The value of 'i' is incremented by 1 after each iteration.

The do-while Loop

The do-while loop is similar to the while loop, but it guarantees that the code block will be executed at least once, even if the condition is false. Here's the basic syntax:

```
do {
  // code to be executed
  } while (condition);
```

For example, let's print the numbers 1 to 5 using a do-while loop:

```
int i = 1;
  do {
  System.out.println(i);
  i++;
  } while (i <= 5);
```

In this example, the code block is executed first, and then the condition 'i <= 5' is checked. If the condition is true, the loop continues.

Break and Continue

The break and continue statements are used to control the flow of loops. The break statement is used to exit the loop prematurely, while the continue statement skips the rest of the code inside the loop for the current iteration and proceeds to the next iteration.

For example, let's use the break statement to exit a loop when a certain condition is met:

```
for (int i = 1; i <= 10; i++) {
  if (i == 5) {
  break;
  }
  System.out.println(i);
  }
```

In this example, the loop prints the numbers 1 to 4. When 'i' equals 5, the break statement is executed, and the loop terminates.

Now, let's use the continue statement to skip the current iteration when a certain condition is met:

```
for (int i = 1; i <= 10; i++) {
  if (i == 5) {
  continue;
  }
  System.out.println(i);
  }
```

In this example, the loop prints the numbers 1 to 10, except for 5. When 'i' equals 5, the continue statement is executed, and the loop proceeds to the next iteration without printing 5.

Real-Life Scenarios

Control flow statements are essential for writing programs that can handle real-life scenarios. For example, consider a simple program that checks the temperature and provides advice based on the value:

```
int temperature = 25;
  if (temperature > 30) {
  System.out.println("It's hot outside! Stay hydrated.");
  } else if (temperature >= 20 && temperature <= 30) {
  System.out.println("The weather is nice and warm.");
  } else {
  System.out.println("It's cold outside! Dress warmly.");
  }
```

In this example, the program uses if, else if, and else statements to provide different messages based on the temperature.

Takeaways

Alright, let's wrap up with some key takeaways from this chapter:
   - Control flow determines the path your program takes as it runs.
   - Conditionals (if, else if, else, and switch) allow your program to execute code blocks based on whether conditions are true or false.
   - Loops (for, while, and do-while) allow your program to execute code blocks repeatedly based on a condition.
   - The break and continue statements are used to control the flow of loops.
   - Understanding control flow is essential for writing dynamic and responsive programs.

By mastering conditionals and loops, you're giving your Java

programs the ability to make decisions and perform repetitive tasks. These skills are fundamental to writing effective and efficient code. Keep practicing and experimenting with different scenarios to reinforce your understanding.

In the next chapter, we'll explore functions and methods, which will help you organize your code into reusable and modular components.

Chapter 5: Functions and Methods

Welcome to Chapter 5! Now that you're familiar with Java syntax, variables, data types, and control flow, it's time to take your programming skills to the next level by learning about functions and methods. These are essential tools that allow you to organize your code into reusable, modular units, making it easier to read, maintain, and debug. Think of functions and methods as the magic spells in your programming spellbook—they can perform tasks, solve problems, and make your code more efficient.

Understanding Functions and Methods

In Java, the terms "function" and "method" are often used interchangeably, but there is a subtle difference. A function is a block of code that performs a specific task, while a method is a function that belongs to a class. Since Java is an object-oriented programming language, we primarily use methods. However, for simplicity, we'll use the terms interchangeably in this chapter.

Why Use Functions and Methods?

Imagine you're writing a program that performs a series of tasks, like calculating the area of different shapes, processing user input, or displaying messages. Without functions and methods, your code would be one long sequence of statements, making it hard to manage and understand. By breaking your code into smaller, reusable units (functions and methods), you can:

  - Simplify complex problems by dividing them into smaller, manageable tasks.

  - Avoid repeating code by reusing functions and methods.

  - Improve readability and maintainability by organizing code logically.

  - Make debugging easier by isolating errors to specific functions or methods.

Defining and Calling Methods

Let's start with the basics of defining and calling methods. Here's the general syntax for defining a method in Java:

```
accessModifier returnType methodName(parameters) {
  // method body
  }
```

Let's break this down:

  - 'accessModifier': Specifies the visibility of the method (e.g., 'public', 'private', 'protected').

  - 'returnType': The type of value the method returns (e.g., 'int', 'String', 'void'). Use 'void' if the method doesn't return a value.

  - 'methodName': The name of the method.

  - 'parameters': A comma-separated list of input parameters (optional).

Here's an example of a simple method that prints a greeting message:

```
public void printGreeting() {
  System.out.println("Hello, welcome to Java programming!");
  }
```

To call this method, simply use its name followed by parentheses:

```
printGreeting();
```

Method Parameters and Return Values

Methods can accept input parameters and return values, allowing them to perform more complex tasks. For example, let's create a method that calculates the sum of two integers:

```
public int sum(int a, int b) {
  return a + b;
  }
```

In this example, the method 'sum' takes two integer parameters ('a' and 'b') and returns their sum. To call this method and store the result in a variable, you would write:

```
int result = sum(5, 3);
  System.out.println("The sum is: " + result);
```

Method Overloading

Method overloading is a feature in Java that allows you to define multiple methods with the same name but different parameter lists. This can be useful when you want to perform similar tasks with different types or numbers of inputs. Here's an example of method overloading:

```
public int sum(int a, int b) {
  return a + b;
  }

public double sum(double a, double b) {
  return a + b;
  }

public int sum(int a, int b, int c) {
```

```
return a + b + c;
}
```

In this example, we have three 'sum' methods: one that takes two integers, one that takes two doubles, and one that takes three integers. Java will automatically select the appropriate method based on the arguments you provide.

Method Recursion

Recursion is a powerful programming technique where a method calls itself to solve a problem. It's often used for tasks that can be broken down into smaller, similar sub-tasks. However, recursion can be tricky to get right and may lead to infinite loops if not handled properly. Here's a simple example of a recursive method that calculates the factorial of a number:

```
public int factorial(int n) {
  if (n <= 1) {
  return 1;
  } else {
  return n * factorial(n - 1);
  }
}
```

In this example, the 'factorial' method calls itself with the value 'n - 1' until 'n' is less than or equal to 1. To calculate the factorial of a number, you would call the method like this:

```
int result = factorial(5);
  System.out.println("The factorial of 5 is: " + result);
```

Real-Life Scenarios

Functions and methods are incredibly useful in real-life programming scenarios. Let's explore a few examples to see how they can simplify your code
and make it more modular.

Example 1: Temperature Conversion

Suppose you're writing a program that converts temperatures between Celsius
and Fahrenheit. Instead of writing the conversion formulas multiple times,
you can create methods to handle the conversions:

```
public double celsiusToFahrenheit(double celsius) {
    return (celsius * 9 / 5) + 32;
    }
```

```
public double fahrenheitToCelsius(double fahrenheit) {
    return (fahrenheit - 32) * 5 / 9;
    }
```

Now, you can easily convert temperatures by calling these methods:

```
double tempC = 25.0;
    double tempF = celsiusToFahrenheit(tempC);
    System.out.println(tempC + "°C is " + tempF + "°F");
```

Example 2: Checking for Prime Numbers

Let's create a method that checks if a number is prime. A prime number is a
number greater than 1 that has no divisors other than 1 and itself:

```
public boolean isPrime(int number) {
    if (number <= 1) {
    return false;
    }
```

```
for (int i = 2; i <= Math.sqrt(number); i++) {
if (number % i == 0) {
return false;
}
}
return true;
}
```

You can use this method to check if a number is prime:

```
int num = 17;
  if (isPrime(num)) {
  System.out.println(num + " is a prime number.");
  } else {
  System.out.println(num + " is not a prime number.");
  }
```

Example 3: Finding the Maximum Value in an Array

Let's write a method that finds the maximum value in an array of integers:

```
public int findMax(int[] array) {
  int max = array[0];
  for (int i = 1; i < array.length; i++) {
  if (array[i] > max) {
  max = array[i];
  }
  }
  return max;
  }
```

You can use this method to find the maximum value in an array:

```
int[] numbers = {3, 5, 7, 2, 8};
    int maxValue = findMax(numbers);
    System.out.println("The maximum value is: " + maxValue);
```

Takeaways

Alright, let's wrap up with some key takeaways from this chapter:
  - Functions and methods are blocks of code that perform specific tasks and can be reused throughout your program.
  - Defining methods involves specifying access modifiers, return types, method names, and parameters.
  - Methods can accept input parameters and return values, allowing them to perform more complex tasks.
  - Method overloading allows you to define multiple methods with the same name but different parameter lists.
  - Recursion is a technique where a method calls itself to solve a problem.
  - Functions and methods simplify your code, improve readability, and make debugging easier.

By mastering functions and methods, you're taking a significant step towards writing more organized and efficient Java programs. These skills are essential for tackling more complex problems and building robust applications. Keep practicing and experimenting with different methods to reinforce your understanding.

In the next chapter, we'll explore object-oriented programming (OOP) concepts, which will help you understand how to design and structure your code using classes and objects.

Chapter 6: Object-Oriented Programming (OOP) Concepts

Welcome to Chapter 6! By now, you've got a good grip on the basics of Java, including syntax, variables, data types, control flow, and methods. It's time to dive into one of the most powerful features of Java: Object-Oriented Programming (OOP). OOP is a programming paradigm that uses "objects" to design applications and programs. Think of it as organizing your code into a collection of interconnected mini-programs that work together to accomplish tasks.

Understanding OOP

At its core, OOP is about modeling real-world entities as software objects that have both state and behavior. The state is represented by the object's attributes (fields or properties), and the behavior is represented by the object's methods. The four main principles of OOP are encapsulation, inheritance, polymorphism, and abstraction. Let's explore each of these concepts in detail.

Encapsulation

Encapsulation is the bundling of data (attributes) and methods that operate on the data into a single unit, known as a class. It also involves restricting direct access to some of an object's components, which is a way of hiding the internal state of the object and only exposing a controlled interface.

Here's an example to illustrate encapsulation:

```
public class Car {
   private String model;
   private int year;

public Car(String model, int year) {
   this.model = model;
   this.year = year;
   }

public String getModel() {
   return model;
   }

public void setModel(String model) {
   this.model = model;
   }

public int getYear() {
   return year;
   }

public void setYear(int year) {
   this.year = year;
   }
   }
```

In this example, the 'Car' class encapsulates the 'model' and 'year' attributes. These attributes are marked as 'private', meaning they cannot be accessed directly from outside the class. Instead, we provide 'public' getter and setter methods to access and modify these attributes. This encapsulation ensures that the internal state of the object is protected from unauthorized access and modification.

Inheritance

Inheritance is a mechanism that allows one class to inherit the properties and methods of another class. The class that inherits is called the subclass (or derived class), and the class being inherited from is called the superclass (or base class). Inheritance promotes code reusability and establishes a natural hierarchy between classes.

Here's an example of inheritance:

```java
public class Vehicle {
    private String brand;

    public Vehicle(String brand) {
        this.brand = brand;
    }

    public String getBrand() {
        return brand;
    }

    public void setBrand(String brand) {
        this.brand = brand;
    }

    public void start() {
        System.out.println("The vehicle is starting.");
    }
}
```

```
public class Car extends Vehicle {
    private int numDoors;

    public Car(String brand, int numDoors) {
        super(brand);
        this.numDoors = numDoors;
    }

    public int getNumDoors() {
        return numDoors;
    }

    public void setNumDoors(int numDoors) {
        this.numDoors = numDoors;
    }

    public void honk() {
        System.out.println("The car is honking.");
    }
}
```

In this example, the 'Car' class inherits from the 'Vehicle' class using the 'extends' keyword. The 'Car' class inherits the 'brand' attribute and 'start' method from the 'Vehicle' class, while also adding its own 'numDoors' attribute and 'honk' method. This relationship allows the 'Car' class to reuse the functionality of the 'Vehicle' class while extending it with additional features.

Polymorphism

Polymorphism allows objects of different classes to be treated as objects of a common superclass. It enables a single method to operate on objects of different types, making code more flexible and extensible. There are two types of polymorphism in Java: compile-time (method overloading) and runtime (method overriding).

Method Overloading

Method overloading occurs when multiple methods in a class have the same name but different parameter lists. This allows methods to perform similar tasks with different inputs.

```
public class MathUtils {
    public int add(int a, int b) {
    return a + b;
    }

public double add(double a, double b) {
    return a + b;
    }
    }
```

In this example, the 'MathUtils' class has two 'add' methods: one that takes two integers and another that takes two doubles. The appropriate method is selected based on the arguments provided at compile time.

Method Overriding

Method overriding occurs when a subclass provides a specific implementation for a method that is already defined in its superclass. This allows the subclass to modify or extend the behavior of the superclass method.

```
public class Animal {
    public void makeSound() {
    System.out.println("The animal makes a sound.");
    }
```

```
}

public class Dog extends Animal {
  @Override
  public void makeSound() {
  System.out.println("The dog barks.");
  }
  }
```

In this example, the 'Dog' class overrides the 'makeSound' method of the 'Animal' class. When 'makeSound' is called on a 'Dog' object, the overridden method in the 'Dog' class is executed, demonstrating runtime polymorphism.

Abstraction

Abstraction is the concept of hiding the complex implementation details of a system and exposing only the necessary features. In Java, abstraction is achieved using abstract classes and interfaces.

Abstract Classes

An abstract class is a class that cannot be instantiated and may contain abstract methods (methods without a body) that must be implemented by subclasses.

```
public abstract class Shape {
   private String color;

public Shape(String color) {
   this.color = color;
   }

public String getColor() {
   return color;
```

```
    }

public void setColor(String color) {
    this.color = color;
    }

public abstract double calculateArea();
    }

public class Circle extends Shape {
    private double radius;

public Circle(String color, double radius) {
    super(color);
    this.radius = radius;
    }

@Override
    public double calculateArea() {
    return Math.PI * radius * radius;
    }
    }
```

In this example, the 'Shape' class is abstract and contains an abstract method 'calculateArea'. The 'Circle' class extends 'Shape' and provides an implementation for the 'calculateArea' method.

Interfaces

An interface is a reference type in Java that is similar to a class but only contains abstract methods (by default) and constants. Interfaces are used to define a contract that implementing classes must fulfill.

```
public interface Drawable {
  void draw();
  }

public class Square implements Drawable {
  @Override
  public void draw() {
  System.out.println("Drawing a square.");
  }
  }
```

In this example, the 'Drawable' interface defines a 'draw' method. The 'Square' class implements the 'Drawable' interface and provides an implementation for the 'draw' method.

Real-Life Scenarios

Object-oriented programming concepts are widely used in real-life scenarios to design and develop software systems. Let's explore a few examples to see how OOP principles can be applied.

Example 1: Library Management System

In a library management system, you can model different entities such as books, members, and loans using classes. For instance, you can create a 'Book' class with attributes like 'title', 'author', and 'ISBN', and methods like 'borrow' and 'returnBook'. You can also create a 'Member' class with attributes like 'name', 'membershipId', and 'borrowedBooks', and methods like 'borrowBook' and 'returnBook'.

By using inheritance, you can create specialized classes for different types of members, such as 'Student' and 'Teacher', each with additional attributes and methods specific to their roles. Polymorphism allows you to handle different types of members uniformly, while encapsulation ensures that the internal state of objects is protected.

Example 2: E-Commerce System

In an e-commerce system, you can use classes to model entities like products, customers, orders, and payments. For example, you can create a 'Product' class with attributes like 'name', 'price', and 'stock', and methods like 'addToCart' and 'removeFromCart'. You can also create an 'Order' class with attributes like 'orderId', 'customer', and 'orderItems', and methods like 'placeOrder' and 'cancelOrder'.

Inheritance allows you to create different types of products, such as 'Electronics' and 'Clothing', each with additional attributes and methods. Interfaces can be used to define contracts for payment processing, with different implementations for credit card payments, PayPal payments, and more.

Takeaways

By understanding and applying the principles of object-oriented programming, you can design and develop software that is modular, reusable, and easier to maintain. OOP concepts like encapsulation, inheritance, polymorphism, and abstraction help you model real-world entities and their interactions in a structured and organized way.

Keep practicing and experimenting with these concepts to reinforce your understanding and improve your programming skills. With a solid grasp of OOP principles, you'll be well-equipped to tackle more complex projects and challenges in the world of Java programming.

Chapter 7: Working with Arrays and Collections

Welcome to Chapter 7! Now that you've got a solid understanding of Java's object-oriented programming principles, it's time to tackle another crucial aspect of programming: handling multiple pieces of data efficiently. Enter arrays and collections. Think of them as tools for organizing, managing, and manipulating groups of related items in your programs. Arrays and collections are like your digital filing cabinets, helping you keep everything neat, tidy, and accessible.

Understanding Arrays

Arrays are the most basic data structure in Java. They are fixed-size, ordered collections of elements of the same type. Imagine you have a row of lockers, each labeled with a number and capable of holding one item. That's essentially what an array is—a series of containers (elements) that can store data, each accessed by an index.

Here's how you declare and initialize an array in Java:

int[] numbers = new int[5]; // Declares an array of integers with 5 elements

You can also initialize an array with values at the time of declaration:

```java
int[] numbers = {1, 2, 3, 4, 5}; // Declares and initializes an array with 5 elements
```

Accessing and Modifying Array Elements

You access elements of an array using their index, which starts at 0. Here's an example of how to access and modify elements in an array:

```java
int firstNumber = numbers[0]; // Accesses the first element
  numbers[1] = 10; // Modifies the second element
```

You can also loop through an array to access or modify its elements. For example, let's print all the elements of the 'numbers' array:

```java
for (int i = 0; i < numbers.length; i++) {
  System.out.println(numbers[i]);
  }
```

This for loop iterates over each element of the array and prints it to the console.

Multidimensional Arrays

Java also supports multidimensional arrays, which are arrays of arrays. These are useful for representing data in a grid or table format. Here's how you declare and initialize a two-dimensional array:

```java
int[][] matrix = {
  {1, 2, 3},
  {4, 5, 6},
  {7, 8, 9}
  };
```

You can access elements in a two-dimensional array using two indices:

int value = matrix[1][2]; // Accesses the element in the second row, third column (value is 6)

Working with Collections

While arrays are useful, they come with limitations, such as fixed size. This is where collections come in. Collections are part of the Java Collections Framework, which provides a set of classes and interfaces for storing and manipulating groups of data more flexibly and efficiently.

The main interfaces in the Java Collections Framework are List, Set, and Map. Let's explore each of these in detail.

The List Interface

A List is an ordered collection that allows duplicate elements. It's like an array, but with dynamic sizing and additional functionality. The most commonly used implementations of the List interface are ArrayList and LinkedList.

Here's an example of how to use an ArrayList:

```
import java.util.ArrayList;
   import java.util.List;

public class Main {
   public static void main(String[] args) {
   List<String> fruits = new ArrayList<>();

// Adding elements
   fruits.add("Apple");
   fruits.add("Banana");
   fruits.add("Orange");
```

```
// Accessing elements
   String firstFruit = fruits.get(0); // Accesses the first element
   System.out.println("First fruit: " + firstFruit);

// Iterating over elements
   for (String fruit : fruits) {
   System.out.println(fruit);
   }

// Modifying elements
   fruits.set(1, "Mango"); // Changes the second element to Mango

// Removing elements
   fruits.remove(0); // Removes the first element (Apple)

System.out.println("Fruits after modifications: " + fruits);
   }
   }
```

In this example, we use an ArrayList to store a list of fruits. We add elements, access and modify them, and iterate over the list to print each element.

The Set Interface

A Set is an unordered collection that does not allow duplicate elements. It's useful when you need to store unique items. The most commonly used implementations of the Set interface are HashSet, LinkedHashSet, and TreeSet.

Here's an example of how to use a HashSet:

```
import java.util.HashSet;
   import java.util.Set;
```

```java
public class Main {
   public static void main(String[] args) {
   Set<String> uniqueFruits = new HashSet<>();

// Adding elements
   uniqueFruits.add("Apple");
   uniqueFruits.add("Banana");
   uniqueFruits.add("Orange");
   uniqueFruits.add("Apple"); // Duplicate element

// Iterating over elements
   for (String fruit : uniqueFruits) {
   System.out.println(fruit);
   }

// Checking if a Set contains an element
   boolean hasBanana = uniqueFruits.contains("Banana");
   System.out.println("Contains Banana: " + hasBanana);

// Removing elements
   uniqueFruits.remove("Orange");

System.out.println("Fruits after modifications: " + uniqueFruits);
   }
   }
```

In this example, we use a HashSet to store a set of unique fruits. Note that adding a duplicate element ("Apple") does not affect the Set.

The Map Interface

A Map is a collection that maps keys to values, with no duplicate keys allowed. It's useful for associating unique keys with specific values. The most commonly used implementations of the Map interface are HashMap, LinkedHashMap, and TreeMap.

Here's an example of how to use a HashMap:

```
import java.util.HashMap;
  import java.util.Map;

public class Main {
  public static void main(String[] args) {
  Map<String, Integer> fruitPrices = new HashMap<>();

// Adding key-value pairs
  fruitPrices.put("Apple", 150);
  fruitPrices.put("Banana", 50);
  fruitPrices.put("Orange", 100);

// Accessing values by key
  int applePrice = fruitPrices.get("Apple");
  System.out.println("Price of Apple: " + applePrice);

// Iterating over key-value pairs
  for (Map.Entry<String, Integer> entry : fruitPrices.entrySet()) {
  System.out.println(entry.getKey() + ": " + entry.getValue());
  }

// Modifying values
  fruitPrices.put("Banana", 60); // Changes the price of Banana to 60

// Removing key-value pairs
  fruitPrices.remove("Orange");

System.out.println("Fruit prices after modifications: " + fruitPrices);
```

```
  }
  }
```

In this example, we use a HashMap to store fruit prices. We add key-value pairs, access values by key, iterate over the entries, and modify and remove elements.

Real-Life Scenarios

Arrays and collections are indispensable in real-life programming scenarios. Let's explore a few examples to see how they can simplify data management and manipulation.

Example 1: Student Grades

Suppose you're writing a program to manage student grades. You can use an ArrayList to store the grades and calculate the average grade:

```java
import java.util.ArrayList;
  import java.util.List;

public class Main {
   public static void main(String[] args) {
   List<Integer> grades = new ArrayList<>();

grades.add(85);
   grades.add(90);
   grades.add(78);
   grades.add(92);

int total = 0;
   for (int grade : grades) {
   total += grade;
```

```
}

double average = total / (double) grades.size();
    System.out.println("Average grade: " + average);
    }
    }
```

In this example, we use an ArrayList to store student grades and calculate the average grade by summing the grades and dividing by the number of grades.

Example 2: Unique Usernames

Suppose you're writing a program that manages user registrations and ensures that usernames are unique. You can use a HashSet to store usernames and check for duplicates:

```
import java.util.HashSet;
    import java.util.Set;

public class Main {
    public static void main(String[] args) {
    Set<String> usernames = new HashSet<>();

usernames.add("john_doe");
    usernames.add("jane_smith");
    usernames.add("john_doe"); // Duplicate username

if (usernames.contains("john_doe")) {
    System.out.println("Username 'john_doe' is already taken.");
    } else {
    usernames.add("john_doe");
    }
```

```
System.out.println("Usernames: " + usernames);
    }
    }
```

In this example, we use a HashSet to store usernames and check if a username is already taken before adding it.

Example 3: Inventory Management

Suppose you're writing an inventory management system for a store. You can use a HashMap to store product names and their quantities:

```
import java.util.HashMap;
    import java.util.Map;

public class Main {
    public static void main(String[] args) {
    Map<String, Integer> inventory = new HashMap<>();

inventory.put("Apples", 50);
    inventory.put("Bananas", 30);
    inventory.put("Oranges", 20);

// Sell some apples
    int applesSold = 10;
    inventory.put("Apples", inventory.get("Apples") - applesSold);

System.out.println("Inventory after sale: " + inventory);
    }
    }
```

In this example, we use a HashMap to store the inventory of products and update the quantities when items are sold.

Takeaways

By understanding and using arrays and collections, you can efficiently manage and manipulate groups of related data in your Java programs. Arrays provide a simple way to store and access fixed-size

collections of elements, while collections offer more flexibility and functionality for dynamic and complex data management.

Keep practicing and experimenting with different arrays and collections to reinforce your understanding and improve your programming skills. With a solid grasp of these data structures, you'll be well-equipped to handle a wide range of programming tasks and challenges in Java.

Chapter 8: Exception Handling

Welcome to Chapter 8! We've journeyed through the land of Java, exploring everything from variables and loops to objects and collections. Now, let's tackle one of the most crucial aspects of programming: making sure our programs can handle unexpected events gracefully. Imagine driving a car without knowing how to deal with a flat tire. That's what programming without exception handling is like—sooner or later, something's going to go wrong, and you'd better be prepared.

Understanding Exceptions

In Java, an exception is an event that disrupts the normal flow of the program. When an exception occurs, the program stops executing normally and jumps to a special block of code to handle the issue. Think of exceptions as Java's way of throwing up a red flag and saying, "Hey, something went wrong here!"

There are two main types of exceptions in Java:
  - Checked exceptions: These are exceptions that the compiler checks at compile-time. You must handle these exceptions using try-catch blocks or declare them in the method signature with the 'throws' keyword.
  - Unchecked exceptions: These are exceptions that occur at runtime and are not checked by the compiler. They include subclasses of 'RuntimeException' and 'Error'.

The most common exceptions you might encounter include:

- 'NullPointerException': When you try to use an object reference that hasn't been initialized.

- 'ArrayIndexOutOfBoundsException': When you try to access an array element with an invalid index.

- 'ArithmeticException': When an illegal arithmetic operation, like division by zero, is performed.

- 'IOException': When an input or output operation fails or is interrupted.

Handling Exceptions with try-catch

The most common way to handle exceptions in Java is by using a try-catch block. The code that might throw an exception is placed inside the 'try' block, and the 'catch' block contains the code to handle the exception. Here's the basic syntax:

```
try {
    // code that might throw an exception
    } catch (ExceptionType e) {
    // code to handle the exception
    }
```

Let's see an example of handling an 'ArithmeticException':

```
public class Main {
    public static void main(String[] args) {
    try {
    int result = 10 / 0; // This will throw an ArithmeticException
    } catch (ArithmeticException e) {
    System.out.println("Cannot divide by zero!");
    }
    }
    }
```

In this example, the division operation inside the 'try' block throws an 'ArithmeticException', which is then caught by the 'catch' block. The message "Cannot divide by zero!" is printed to the console, and the program continues to run normally.

Multiple catch Blocks

Sometimes, a block of code might throw more than one type of exception. In such cases, you can use multiple 'catch' blocks to handle different exceptions separately. Here's an example:

```
public class Main {
    public static void main(String[] args) {
    try {
    int[] numbers = {1, 2, 3};
    int result = numbers[5]; // This will throw an ArrayIndexOutOfBoundsExce
ption
    } catch (ArrayIndexOutOfBoundsException e) {
    System.out.println("Array index is out of bounds!");
    } catch (Exception e) {
    System.out.println("An unexpected error occurred: " + e.getMessage());
    }
    }
}
```

In this example, the first 'catch' block handles 'ArrayIndexOutOfBoundsException', and the second 'catch' block handles any other type of exception that might occur.

The finally Block

Sometimes, you need to execute some code regardless of whether an exception was thrown or not. This is where the 'finally' block comes in. The 'finally' block is always executed after the 'try' and 'catch' blocks, even if an exception is thrown. It's typically used for cleanup activities, such as closing files or releasing resources. Here's an example:

```
public class Main {
    public static void main(String[] args) {
    try {
    int result = 10 / 0; // This will throw an ArithmeticException
    } catch (ArithmeticException e) {
    System.out.println("Cannot divide by zero!");
    } finally {
    System.out.println("This will always be executed.");
    }
    }
    }
```

In this example, the 'finally' block prints "This will always be executed." to the console, regardless of whether an exception was thrown or not.

Throwing Exceptions

In addition to catching exceptions, you can also throw exceptions manually using the 'throw' keyword. This is useful when you want to signal that an error has occurred in your method. Here's an example:

```
public class Main {
    public static void main(String[] args) {
    try {
    checkAge(15); // This will throw an IllegalArgumentException
    } catch (IllegalArgumentException e) {
    System.out.println("Caught an exception: " + e.getMessage());
    }
    }
```

```
public static void checkAge(int age) {
  if (age < 18) {
  throw new IllegalArgumentException("Age must be 18 or older.");
  }
  }
  }
```

In this example, the 'checkAge' method throws an 'IllegalArgumentException' if the 'age' parameter is less than 18. The exception is then caught in the 'main' method.

Declaring Exceptions with throws

When a method might throw a checked exception that it does not handle itself, it must declare the exception using the 'throws' keyword in its method signature. This informs the calling method that it needs to handle the exception. Here's an example:

```
import java.io.BufferedReader;
  import java.io.FileReader;
  import java.io.IOException;

public class Main {
  public static void main(String[] args) {
  try {
  readFile("test.txt");
  } catch (IOException e) {
  System.out.println("Caught an exception: " + e.getMessage());
  }
  }

public static void readFile(String fileName) throws IOException {
  BufferedReader reader = new BufferedReader(new FileReader(fileName));
```

```
String line;
while ((line = reader.readLine()) != null) {
System.out.println(line);
}
reader.close();
}
}
```

In this example, the 'readFile' method declares that it throws an 'IOException'. The 'main' method is responsible for handling this exception.

Custom Exceptions

In addition to using Java's built-in exceptions, you can create your own custom exceptions. This is useful when you need to handle specific error conditions in your application. To create a custom exception, simply extend the 'Exception' class (or any of its subclasses). Here's an example:

```
public class Main {
  public static void main(String[] args) {
  try {
  validateUser("guest");
  } catch (InvalidUserException e) {
  System.out.println("Caught an exception: " + e.getMessage());
  }
  }

public static void validateUser(String userRole) throws InvalidUserException
{
  if (!userRole.equals("admin")) {
  throw new InvalidUserException("User is not authorized.");
  }
  }
```

```
}

class InvalidUserException extends Exception {
   public InvalidUserException(String message) {
   super(message);
   }
   }
```

In this example, we create a custom exception called 'InvalidUserException'
to handle unauthorized user access.

Real-Life Scenarios

Exception handling is essential in real-life programming scenarios to ensure
your applications run smoothly and gracefully handle errors. Let's explore a
few examples to see how exception handling can be applied.

Example 1: File Operations

Suppose you're writing a program to read and process data from a file. Without
exception handling, your program might crash if the file doesn't exist or if
there's an issue reading the file. By using exception handling, you can provide
meaningful error messages and ensure the program continues running:

```
import java.io.BufferedReader;
   import java.io.FileReader;
   import java.io.IOException;

public class Main {
   public static void main(String[] args) {
   String fileName = "data.txt";
   try {
   BufferedReader reader = new BufferedReader(new FileReader(fileName));
```

```
String line;
while ((line = reader.readLine()) != null) {
System.out.println(line);
}
reader.close();
} catch (IOException e) {
System.out.println("Error reading file: " + e.getMessage());
}
}
}
```

Example 2: User Input Validation

When dealing with user input, it's important to validate the input and handle any invalid data gracefully. Here's an example of a program that prompts the user for a number and handles invalid input using exception handling:

```
import java.util.InputMismatchException;
import java.util.Scanner;

public class Main {
public static void main(String[] args) {
Scanner scanner = new Scanner(System.in);
System.out.print("Enter a number: ");
try {
int number = scanner.nextInt();
System.out.println("You entered: " + number);
} catch (InputMismatchException e) {
System.out.println("Invalid input! Please enter a valid number.");
}
}
}
```

Example 3: Network Operations

When writing programs that involve network operations, such as connecting to a server or downloading data, it's important to handle potential errors like connection timeouts or unreachable hosts. Here's an example:

```java
import java.io.IOException;
    import java.net.HttpURLConnection;
    import java.net.URL;

public class Main {
    public static void main(String[] args) {
    String urlString = "http://example.com";
    try {
    URL url = new URL(urlString);
    HttpURLConnection connection = (HttpURLConnection) url.openConnec-
tion();
    connection.setRequestMethod("GET");
    int responseCode = connection.getResponseCode();
    System.out.println("Response Code: " + responseCode);
    } catch (IOException e) {
    System.out.println("Network error: " + e.getMessage());
    }
    }
    }
```

Takeaways

By mastering exception handling, you can write more robust and reliable Java programs that gracefully handle

errors and unexpected events. Exception handling allows you to manage and respond to runtime anomalies, ensuring your applications remain stable and user-friendly.

Keep practicing and experimenting with different exception handling techniques to reinforce your understanding and improve your programming skills. With a solid grasp of exception handling, you'll be well-equipped to build resilient and fault-tolerant Java applications.

Chapter 9: Working with Files and I/O

Welcome to Chapter 9! By now, you've become quite the Java aficionado, tackling everything from object-oriented programming to exception handling. Now it's time to delve into a topic that's essential for any real-world application: working with files and input/output (I/O). Imagine writing a fantastic piece of software that can't save data or read from a file—pretty limiting, right? This chapter will teach you how to handle files and perform I/O operations in Java, making your programs more versatile and functional.

Understanding Java I/O

Java provides a robust and flexible I/O framework that allows you to read from and write to various data sources, such as files, network connections, and even the console. The java.io package contains all the necessary classes and interfaces for handling I/O operations. At the heart of Java's I/O system are streams, which are sequences of data. There are two main types of streams: byte streams and character streams.

Byte Streams vs. Character Streams

Byte streams handle raw binary data and are useful for reading and writing binary files like images or executable files. They use the InputStream and OutputStream classes and their subclasses. Character streams, on the other hand, handle text data and are designed for reading and writing characters.

They use the Reader and Writer classes and their subclasses.

Let's start with some basic file operations, focusing on both byte streams and character streams to give you a well-rounded understanding.

Reading from a File

Reading data from a file is a common task, and Java makes it relatively straightforward. Let's start with an example using byte streams to read a file:

```java
import java.io.FileInputStream;
import java.io.IOException;

public class Main {
    public static void main(String[] args) {
    try (FileInputStream fis = new FileInputStream("example.txt")) {
    int content;
    while ((content = fis.read()) != -1) {
    System.out.print((char) content);
    }
    } catch (IOException e) {
    e.printStackTrace();
    }
    }
    }
```

In this example, we use FileInputStream to read a file named "example.txt" byte by byte. The FileInputStream class reads bytes from a file and returns them as integers. We cast these integers to characters and print them to the console. Notice the try-with-resources statement, which ensures that the FileInputStream is closed automatically at the end of the block, even if an exception occurs.

Now let's read from a file using character streams:

```
import java.io.FileReader;
import java.io.IOException;

public class Main {
    public static void main(String[] args) {
        try (FileReader fr = new FileReader("example.txt")) {
            int content;
            while ((content = fr.read()) != -1) {
                System.out.print((char) content);
            }
        } catch (IOException e) {
            e.printStackTrace();
        }
    }
}
```

In this example, we use FileReader to read the file "example.txt" character by character. FileReader is designed for reading text files and handles character encoding automatically.

Writing to a File

Writing data to a file is just as important as reading from it. Let's start with an example using byte streams to write to a file:

```
import java.io.FileOutputStream;
import java.io.IOException;

public class Main {
    public static void main(String[] args) {
        try (FileOutputStream fos = new FileOutputStream("output.txt")) {
```

```
String data = "Hello, Java!";
fos.write(data.getBytes());
} catch (IOException e) {
e.printStackTrace();
}
}
}
```

In this example, we use FileOutputStream to write the string "Hello, Java!" to a file named "output.txt". The write method writes bytes to the file, so we convert the string to a byte array using the getBytes method.

Now let's write to a file using character streams:

```
import java.io.FileWriter;
  import java.io.IOException;

public class Main {
  public static void main(String[] args) {
  try (FileWriter fw = new FileWriter("output.txt")) {
  String data = "Hello, Java!";
  fw.write(data);
  } catch (IOException e) {
  e.printStackTrace();
  }
  }
}
```

In this example, we use FileWriter to write the string "Hello, Java!" to a file named "output.txt". FileWriter handles character encoding automatically, making it a convenient choice for writing text files.

Buffered Streams

Buffered streams are wrappers around byte and character streams that improve performance by reducing the number of I/O operations. They use an internal buffer to read and write data in larger chunks, which is more efficient than handling one byte or character at a time.

Here's an example of reading from a file using a BufferedInputStream:

```java
import java.io.BufferedInputStream;
import java.io.FileInputStream;
import java.io.IOException;

public class Main {
    public static void main(String[] args) {
    try (BufferedInputStream bis = new BufferedInputStream(new FileInput-
Stream("example.txt"))) {
    int content;
    while ((content = bis.read()) != -1) {
    System.out.print((char) content);
    }
    } catch (IOException e) {
    e.printStackTrace();
    }
    }
}
```

In this example, we wrap a FileInputStream with a BufferedInputStream, which reads data in larger chunks, improving performance.

Here's an example of writing to a file using a BufferedOutputStream:

```java
import java.io.BufferedOutputStream;
import java.io.FileOutputStream;
import java.io.IOException;
```

```java
public class Main {
    public static void main(String[] args) {
    try (BufferedOutputStream bos = new BufferedOutputStream(new FileOut-
putStream("output.txt"))) {
    String data = "Hello, Java!";
    bos.write(data.getBytes());
    } catch (IOException e) {
    e.printStackTrace();
    }
    }
    }
```

In this example, we wrap a FileOutputStream with a BufferedOutputStream, which writes data in larger chunks, improving performance.

File and Directory Operations

Java provides the File class for working with files and directories. The File class offers methods for creating, deleting, and querying files and directories. Here's an example of how to use the File class:

```java
import java.io.File;
    import java.io.IOException;
```

```java
public class Main {
    public static void main(String[] args) {
    File file = new File("newfile.txt");
```

```java
// Create a new file
    try {
    if (file.createNewFile()) {
    System.out.println("File created: " + file.getName());
    } else {
```

```
    System.out.println("File already exists.");
    }
    } catch (IOException e) {
    e.printStackTrace();
    }

// Check if the file exists
    if (file.exists()) {
    System.out.println("File exists: " + file.getName());
    }

// Get file information
    System.out.println("Absolute path: " + file.getAbsolutePath());
    System.out.println("Writable: " + file.canWrite());
    System.out.println("Readable: " + file.canRead());
    System.out.println("File size in bytes: " + file.length());

// Delete the file
    if (file.delete()) {
    System.out.println("File deleted: " + file.getName());
    } else {
    System.out.println("Failed to delete the file.");
    }

// Working with directories
    File dir = new File("myDirectory");

// Create a new directory
    if (dir.mkdir()) {
    System.out.println("Directory created: " + dir.getName());
    } else {
    System.out.println("Failed to create the directory.");
    }
```

```
// List files in a directory
    String[] files = dir.list();
    if (files != null) {
    for (String filename : files) {
    System.out.println("File: " + filename);
    }
    } else {
    System.out.println("Directory is empty or does not exist.");
    }
    }
    }
```

In this example, we use the File class to create, check, and delete a file, as well as create a directory and list its contents. The File class provides a wide range of methods for file and directory manipulation, making it a versatile tool for handling file operations.

Reading and Writing Text Files with BufferedReader and BufferedWriter

When working with text files, using BufferedReader and BufferedWriter can make reading and writing more efficient and convenient. Here's an example of reading a text file using BufferedReader:

```
import java.io.BufferedReader;
    import java.io.FileReader;
    import java.io.IOException;

public class Main {
    public static void main(String[] args) {
    try (BufferedReader br = new BufferedReader(new FileReader("example.txt"))) {
    String line;
    while ((line = br.readLine()) != null) {
```

```
System.out.println(line);
}
} catch (IOException e) {
e.printStackTrace();
}
}
}
```

In this example, we use BufferedReader to read the file "example.txt" line by line, making it easier to handle text files with multiple lines.

Here's an example of writing to a text file using BufferedWriter:

```
import java.io.BufferedWriter;
  import java.io.FileWriter;
  import java.io.IOException;

public class Main {
  public static void main(String[] args) {
  try (BufferedWriter bw = new BufferedWriter(new FileWriter("out-
put.txt"))) {
  String data = "Hello, Java!";
  bw.write(data);
  bw.newLine(); // Add a new line
  bw.write("This is another line.");
  } catch (IOException e) {
  e.printStackTrace();
  }
  }
}
```

In this example, we use BufferedWriter to write the string "Hello, Java!" and another line of text to the file "output.txt". The newLine method adds a line break, making it easy to write multiple lines to a file.

Real-Life Scenarios

File and I

/O operations are essential in many real-life programming scenarios. Let's explore a few examples to see how file handling can be applied.

Example 1: Logging System

A logging system is crucial for debugging and monitoring applications. You can use file handling to create a simple logging system that writes log messages to a file:

```
import java.io.BufferedWriter;
   import java.io.FileWriter;
   import java.io.IOException;
   import java.time.LocalDateTime;
   import java.time.format.DateTimeFormatter;

public class Logger {
   private static final String LOG_FILE = "app.log";

public static void log(String message) {
   try (BufferedWriter bw = new BufferedWriter(new FileWriter(LOG_FILE,
true))) {
   String timestamp = LocalDateTime.now().format(DateTimeFormatter.of-
Pattern("yyyy-MM-dd HH:mm:ss"));
   bw.write(timestamp + " - " + message);
   bw.newLine();
   } catch (IOException e) {
   e.printStackTrace();
```

```
    }
   }
  }
```

```java
public class Main {
  public static void main(String[] args) {
  Logger.log("Application started.");
  Logger.log("An error occurred.");
  Logger.log("Application finished.");
  }
 }
```

In this example, we create a Logger class that writes log messages to a file named "app.log". The log method appends a timestamp to each message, providing a simple way to track events and errors in your application.

Example 2: Configuration Files

Many applications use configuration files to store settings and preferences. You can use file handling to read and write configuration files, allowing users to customize their experience:

```java
import java.io.BufferedReader;
  import java.io.BufferedWriter;
  import java.io.FileReader;
  import java.io.FileWriter;
  import java.io.IOException;
  import java.util.HashMap;
  import java.util.Map;

public class ConfigManager {
  private static final String CONFIG_FILE = "config.txt";
  private Map<String, String> config = new HashMap<>();
```

```java
public void loadConfig() {
  try (BufferedReader br = new BufferedReader(new FileReader(CON-
FIG_FILE))) {
  String line;
  while ((line = br.readLine()) != null) {
  String[] parts = line.split("=");
  if (parts.length == 2) {
  config.put(parts[0], parts[1]);
  }
  }
  } catch (IOException e) {
  e.printStackTrace();
  }
  }

public void saveConfig() {
  try (BufferedWriter bw = new BufferedWriter(new FileWriter(CON-
FIG_FILE))) {
  for (Map.Entry<String, String> entry : config.entrySet()) {
  bw.write(entry.getKey() + "=" + entry.getValue());
  bw.newLine();
  }
  } catch (IOException e) {
  e.printStackTrace();
  }
  }

public String getConfig(String key) {
  return config.get(key);
  }

public void setConfig(String key, String value) {
  config.put(key, value);
```

```java
    }
}

public class Main {
    public static void main(String[] args) {
    ConfigManager configManager = new ConfigManager();
    configManager.loadConfig();

String theme = configManager.getConfig("theme");
    System.out.println("Current theme: " + theme);

configManager.setConfig("theme", "dark");
    configManager.saveConfig();
    }
}
```

In this example, we create a ConfigManager class that reads and writes configuration settings to a file named "config.txt". The loadConfig method loads the configuration from the file into a Map, and the saveConfig method writes the configuration to the file. This allows you to easily manage application settings.

Example 3: Data Processing

Suppose you're writing a program that processes data from a CSV file. You can use file handling to read the CSV file, process the data, and write the results to a new file:

```java
import java.io.BufferedReader;
    import java.io.BufferedWriter;
    import java.io.FileReader;
    import java.io.FileWriter;
    import java.io.IOException;
```

```
public class DataProcessor {
    public static void main(String[] args) {
    String inputFile = "data.csv";
    String outputFile = "results.csv";

try (BufferedReader br = new BufferedReader(new FileReader(inputFile));
    BufferedWriter bw = new BufferedWriter(new FileWriter(outputFile))) {

String line;
    while ((line = br.readLine()) != null) {
    String[] parts = line.split(",");
    // Process data (for example, calculate sum of values)
    int sum = 0;
    for (String part : parts) {
    sum += Integer.parseInt(part);
    }
    bw.write("Sum: " + sum);
    bw.newLine();
    }
    } catch (IOException e) {
    e.printStackTrace();
    }
    }
    }
```

In this example, we read a CSV file named "data.csv", process each line to calculate the sum of values, and write the results to a new file named "results.csv". This demonstrates how file handling can be used for data processing tasks.

Takeaways

By mastering file and I/O operations, you can create more versatile and functional Java programs that can read from and write to various data sources. Understanding the differences between byte streams and character streams, as well as how to use buffered streams for improved performance, will help you handle files and data efficiently. File handling is essential for tasks such as logging, configuration management, and data processing, making it a vital skill for any Java programmer.

Keep practicing and experimenting with different file and I/O operations to reinforce your understanding and improve your programming skills. With a solid grasp of these concepts, you'll be well-equipped to build robust and flexible Java applications.

Chapter 10: Basic Java APIs and Libraries

Welcome to Chapter 10! You've made it this far, and now it's time to dive into some of the powerful APIs and libraries that Java provides. These tools are like secret weapons in your programming arsenal, enabling you to accomplish complex tasks with relative ease. From handling dates and times to manipulating collections and performing I/O operations, Java's standard library has got you covered.

Understanding the Java Standard Library

The Java Standard Library is a vast collection of classes and interfaces that provide essential functionality for everyday programming tasks. It's organized into packages, each serving a different purpose. Some of the most commonly used packages include:

- java.lang: Provides fundamental classes, such as String, Math, and System.
- java.util: Contains utility classes, such as collections, date and time facilities, and random number generators.
- java.io: Provides classes for input and output operations, including file handling.
- java.nio: Offers classes for non-blocking I/O operations.
- java.net: Contains classes for networking, such as URL, Socket, and ServerSocket.
- java.time: Introduces the new date and time API, which is more powerful and flexible than the old java.util.Date and java.util.Calendar classes.

Let's explore some of the most useful APIs and libraries in the Java Standard Library and see how they can make your life easier as a programmer.

The java.lang Package

The java.lang package is automatically imported into every Java program, so you don't need to import it explicitly. It contains essential classes and interfaces that are fundamental to the Java programming language.

The String Class

The String class is one of the most commonly used classes in Java. It represents a sequence of characters and provides various methods for manipulating strings. Here's an example of how to use the String class:

```java
public class Main {
    public static void main(String[] args) {
    String greeting = "Hello, Java!";

// Length of the string
    int length = greeting.length();
    System.out.println("Length: " + length);

// Character at a specific index
    char firstChar = greeting.charAt(0);
    System.out.println("First character: " + firstChar);

// Substring
    String substring = greeting.substring(7, 11);
    System.out.println("Substring: " + substring);

// Replace
    String newGreeting = greeting.replace("Java", "World");
```

```
System.out.println("New greeting: " + newGreeting);
    }
}
```

In this example, we use various methods of the String class to manipulate the string "Hello, Java!" and print the results.

The Math Class

The Math class provides methods for performing basic numeric operations, such as arithmetic, trigonometry, and logarithms. Here's an example of how to use the Math class:

```
public class Main {
    public static void main(String[] args) {
        double number = 25.0;

// Square root
        double sqrt = Math.sqrt(number);
        System.out.println("Square root: " + sqrt);

// Power
        double power = Math.pow(number, 2);
        System.out.println("Power: " + power);

// Maximum and minimum
        double max = Math.max(number, 30.0);
        double min = Math.min(number, 20.0);
        System.out.println("Max: " + max);
        System.out.println("Min: " + min);

// Random number
        double random = Math.random();
```

```
System.out.println("Random number: " + random);
}
}
```

In this example, we use various methods of the Math class to perform mathematical operations and print the results.

The java.util Package

The java.util package contains utility classes that provide essential functionality for collections, date and time handling, and more.

The Collections Framework

The Collections Framework provides a set of classes and interfaces for working with groups of objects. It includes classes like ArrayList, HashSet, and HashMap, which we've already explored. Let's look at some additional functionality provided by the Collections class:

```
import java.util.ArrayList;
  import java.util.Collections;
  import java.util.List;

public class Main {
  public static void main(String[] args) {
  List<Integer> numbers = new ArrayList<>();
  numbers.add(3);
  numbers.add(1);
  numbers.add(4);
  numbers.add(1);
  numbers.add(5);

// Sort the list
```

```
Collections.sort(numbers);
System.out.println("Sorted list: " + numbers);

// Reverse the list
Collections.reverse(numbers);
System.out.println("Reversed list: " + numbers);

// Find the maximum and minimum elements
int max = Collections.max(numbers);
int min = Collections.min(numbers);
System.out.println("Max: " + max);
System.out.println("Min: " + min);

// Shuffle the list
Collections.shuffle(numbers);
System.out.println("Shuffled list: " + numbers);
    }
}
```

In this example, we use the Collections class to sort, reverse, find the maximum and minimum elements, and shuffle a list of numbers.

The Date and Time API

The java.time package introduces a modern and comprehensive date and time API. It provides classes like LocalDate, LocalTime, and LocalDateTime, which are immutable and thread-safe. Here's an example of how to use the new date and time API:

```
import java.time.LocalDate;
import java.time.LocalTime;
import java.time.LocalDateTime;
import java.time.format.DateTimeFormatter;
```

```
public class Main {
    public static void main(String[] args) {
    // Current date
    LocalDate currentDate = LocalDate.now();
    System.out.println("Current date: " + currentDate);

// Current time
    LocalTime currentTime = LocalTime.now();
    System.out.println("Current time: " + currentTime);

// Current date and time
    LocalDateTime currentDateTime = LocalDateTime.now();
    System.out.println("Current date and time: " + currentDateTime);

// Formatting date and time
    DateTimeFormatter formatter = DateTimeFormatter.ofPattern("yyyy-MM-
dd HH:mm:ss");
    String formattedDateTime = currentDateTime.format(formatter);
    System.out.println("Formatted date and time: " + formattedDateTime);

// Parsing date and time
    String dateTimeString = "2024-01-01 12:00:00";
    LocalDateTime parsedDateTime = LocalDateTime.parse(dateTimeString,
formatter);
    System.out.println("Parsed date and time: " + parsedDateTime);
    }
    }
```

In this example, we use various classes from the java.time package to work with dates and times, format them, and parse them from strings.

The java.io Package

The java.io package provides classes for input and output operations, including file handling. We've already explored file reading and writing in the previous chapter. Let's look at an example of using ObjectInputStream and ObjectOutputStream to serialize and deserialize objects:

```
import java.io.*;

class Person implements Serializable {
    private static final long serialVersionUID = 1L;
    private String name;
    private int age;

public Person(String name, int age) {
    this.name = name;
    this.age = age;
    }

@Override
    public String toString() {
    return "Person{name='" + name + "', age=" + age + '}';
    }
    }

public class Main {
    public static void main(String[] args) {
    Person person = new Person("John Doe", 30);

// Serialize the object
    try (ObjectOutputStream oos = new ObjectOutputStream(new FileOutputStream("person.ser"))) {
    oos.writeObject(person);
    System.out.println("Object serialized: " + person);
    } catch (IOException e) {
```

```
e.printStackTrace();
}
```

```
// Deserialize the object
    try (ObjectInputStream ois = new ObjectInputStream(new FileInput-
Stream("person.ser"))) {
    Person deserializedPerson = (Person) ois.readObject();
    System.out.println("Object deserialized: " + deserializedPerson);
    } catch (IOException | ClassNotFoundException e) {
    e.printStackTrace();
    }
    }
    }
```

In this example, we create a Person class that implements the Serializable interface, allowing it to be serialized and deserialized. We use ObjectOutput-Stream to write the object to a file and ObjectInputStream to read the object from the file.

The java.net Package

The java.net package provides classes for networking, such as URL, Socket, and ServerSocket. Here's an example of how to use the URL class to read the content of a web page:

```
import java.io.BufferedReader;
    import java.io.InputStreamReader;
    import java.net.URL;
```

```
public class Main {
    public static void main(String[] args) {
    try {
    URL url = new URL("http://example.com");
```

```
BufferedReader reader = new BufferedReader(new InputStreamReader(url.open-
Stream()));
String line;
while ((line = reader.readLine()) != null) {
System.out.println(line);
}
reader.close();
} catch (Exception e) {
e.printStackTrace();
}
}
}
```

In this example, we use the URL class to open a connection to a web page and read its content line by line using BufferedReader.

The java.nio Package

The java.nio (New I/O) package provides classes for non-blocking I/O operations, which can improve performance in certain scenarios. Here's an example of using the Files class from java.nio.file to read and write files:

```
import java.nio.file.Files;
import java.nio.file.Paths;
import java.util.List;

public class Main {
public static void main(String[] args) {
String filePath = "example.txt";
List<String> lines;

// Read all lines from a file
try {
```

```
    lines = Files

.readAllLines(Paths.get(filePath));
    for (String line : lines) {
    System.out.println(line);
    }
    } catch (Exception e) {
    e.printStackTrace();
    }

// Write lines to a file
    try {
    List<String> newLines = List.of("Hello, Java NIO!", "This is a new line.");
    Files.write(Paths.get("output.txt"), newLines);
    } catch (Exception e) {
    e.printStackTrace();
    }
    }
    }
```

In this example, we use the Files class to read all lines from a file and write new lines to a different file.

Real-Life Scenarios

Using Java APIs and libraries can significantly simplify various real-life programming tasks. Let's explore a few examples.

Example 1: Data Encryption

Suppose you're writing an application that needs to encrypt sensitive data. You can use the javax.crypto package to perform encryption and decryption:

```java
import javax.crypto.Cipher;
import javax.crypto.KeyGenerator;
import javax.crypto.SecretKey;
import java.util.Base64;

public class Main {
    public static void main(String[] args) {
        try {
            // Generate a secret key
            KeyGenerator keyGen = KeyGenerator.getInstance("AES");
            keyGen.init(128);
            SecretKey secretKey = keyGen.generateKey();

            // Encrypt the data
            Cipher cipher = Cipher.getInstance("AES");
            cipher.init(Cipher.ENCRYPT_MODE, secretKey);
            String originalData = "Sensitive Data";
            byte[] encryptedData = cipher.doFinal(originalData.getBytes());
            String encodedEncryptedData = Base64.getEncoder().encodeToString(encryptedData);
            System.out.println("Encrypted Data: " + encodedEncryptedData);

            // Decrypt the data
            cipher.init(Cipher.DECRYPT_MODE, secretKey);
            byte[] decryptedData = cipher.doFinal(Base64.getDecoder().decode(encodedEncryptedData));
            String decryptedString = new String(decryptedData);
            System.out.println("Decrypted Data: " + decryptedString);
        } catch (Exception e) {
            e.printStackTrace();
        }
    }
}
```

In this example, we use the javax.crypto package to generate a secret key, encrypt data using AES encryption, and then decrypt the data back to its original form.

Example 2: JSON Parsing

Suppose you're writing an application that needs to parse JSON data. You can use the org.json library to parse and manipulate JSON:

import org.json.JSONObject;

```
public class Main {
    public static void main(String[] args) {
    String jsonString = "{\"name\":\"John Doe\",\"age\":30,\"city\":\"New York\"}";
```

```
// Parse the JSON string
    JSONObject jsonObject = new JSONObject(jsonString);
    String name = jsonObject.getString("name");
    int age = jsonObject.getInt("age");
    String city = jsonObject.getString("city");
```

```
System.out.println("Name: " + name);
    System.out.println("Age: " + age);
    System.out.println("City: " + city);
```

```
// Modify the JSON object
    jsonObject.put("age", 31);
    System.out.println("Updated JSON: " + jsonObject.toString());
    }
    }
```

In this example, we use the org.json library to parse a JSON string, extract values, and modify the JSON object.

Example 3: Sending Emails

Suppose you're writing an application that needs to send emails. You can use the javax.mail package to send emails:

```java
import javax.mail.*;
  import javax.mail.internet.InternetAddress;
  import javax.mail.internet.MimeMessage;
  import java.util.Properties;

public class Main {
  public static void main(String[] args) {
  String to = "recipient@example.com";
  String from = "sender@example.com";
  String host = "smtp.example.com";

// Get system properties
  Properties properties = System.getProperties();

// Setup mail server
  properties.setProperty("mail.smtp.host", host);

// Get the default Session object
  Session session = Session.getDefaultInstance(properties);

try {
  // Create a default MimeMessage object
  MimeMessage message = new MimeMessage(session);

// Set From: header field
  message.setFrom(new InternetAddress(from));
```

```java
// Set To: header field
message.addRecipient(Message.RecipientType.TO,    new    InternetAd-
dress(to));

// Set Subject: header field
message.setSubject("This is the Subject Line!");

// Set the actual message
message.setText("This is the actual message");

// Send message
Transport.send(message);
System.out.println("Sent message successfully....");
} catch (MessagingException mex) {
mex.printStackTrace();
}
}
}
```

In this example, we use the javax.mail package to send an email from a specified sender to a specified recipient using an SMTP server.

Takeaways

By mastering Java APIs and libraries, you can leverage powerful tools to simplify complex tasks and enhance your applications. Understanding how to use essential packages like java.lang, java.util, java.io, java.nio, and java.net, as well as additional libraries for encryption, JSON parsing, and email handling, will significantly improve your programming skills. Keep exploring and experimenting with different APIs and libraries to unlock the full potential of Java and build robust, versatile applications.

Conclusion: Your Journey in Java Programming

Congratulations! You've reached the end of this book, but in many ways, it's just the beginning of your adventure in Java programming. We've covered a lot of ground together, from setting up your environment to diving deep into object-oriented programming and exploring the powerful Java APIs. Now, let's take a moment to reflect on what you've learned, what you can do next, and how you can continue to grow as a Java developer.

Looking Back

When you first opened this book, you might have been a bit overwhelmed by the vast world of programming. Maybe you were wondering if you could ever understand all the strange syntax and complex concepts. But look at you now! You've written your first Java programs, handled user input, worked with arrays and collections, and even tackled exception handling. You've mastered the essentials of Java, and that's no small feat.

Think back to the first "Hello, World!" program you wrote. It might seem trivial now, but that simple program was your gateway into the world of coding. From there, you learned about variables, data types, and control flow, which allowed you to write more dynamic and responsive programs. Functions and methods helped you break down complex problems into manageable pieces, and object-oriented programming gave you the tools to create well-structured and reusable code.

Handling files and I/O operations opened up new possibilities for storing and processing data, while understanding Java's rich set of APIs and libraries empowered you to perform complex tasks with ease. Each chapter built upon the previous one, gradually increasing your confidence and competence as a Java programmer.

Where to Go from Here

Now that you have a solid foundation in Java, you might be wondering, "What's next?" The answer depends on your interests and goals. Here are a few paths you can explore to continue your journey:

1. Build Projects: One of the best ways to solidify your knowledge and gain practical experience is by building your own projects. Start small with simple applications like a to-do list or a calculator. Then, challenge yourself with more complex projects like a weather app, a blog, or a game. The more you build, the more you'll learn.

2. Contribute to Open Source: Joining an open-source project is a great way to improve your skills and collaborate with other developers. You'll get to see how large projects are structured, learn best practices, and contribute to something meaningful. Platforms like GitHub and GitLab host thousands of open-source projects looking for contributors.

3. Learn Advanced Topics: Once you're comfortable with the basics, you can start exploring more advanced topics. This could include multi-threading and concurrency, network programming, or even diving into frameworks like Spring and Hibernate. Advanced topics will deepen your understanding of Java and prepare you for more complex tasks.

4. Join a Community: Programming can sometimes feel like a solitary activity, but there are vibrant communities out there. Join online forums, attend meetups, or participate in coding challenges. Engaging with other developers will expose you to new ideas, help you solve problems, and keep you motivated.

5. Prepare for Certification: If you're looking to validate your skills and improve your job prospects, consider preparing for Java certification exams, such as the Oracle Certified Associate (OCA) and Oracle Certified Professional (OCP) certifications. These certifications demonstrate your expertise and can give you an edge in the job market.

6. Read More Books: There are countless books on Java and software development. Some classics include "Effective Java" by Joshua Bloch, "Java Concurrency in Practice" by Brian Goetz, and "Design Patterns" by Erich Gamma et al. These books will deepen your knowledge and introduce you to advanced techniques and best practices.

Practical Tips for Continuous Learning

As you continue your journey, here are some practical tips to keep in mind:

- Practice Regularly: Like any skill, programming requires regular practice. Try to code every day, even if it's just for a short period. Consistent practice will reinforce your learning and help you retain new information.
    - Break Down Problems: When faced with a complex problem, break it down into smaller, manageable pieces. Tackle each piece one at a time, and don't be afraid to iterate and refine your approach.
    - Read Code: Reading other people's code is a great way to learn new techniques and improve your own coding style. Explore open-source projects, read tutorials, and study code samples to see how experienced developers solve problems.
    - Write Tests: Writing tests for your code helps ensure it works correctly and makes it easier to maintain and refactor. Get into the habit of writing unit

tests, integration tests, and other types of tests as part of your development process.

- Seek Feedback: Don't be afraid to ask for feedback on your code. Join coding forums, participate in code reviews, and seek advice from more experienced developers. Constructive feedback can help you identify areas for improvement and learn new approaches.

Staying Motivated

Learning to program can be challenging, and there will be times when you feel stuck or frustrated. Here are some tips to stay motivated and keep making progress:

- Set Goals: Setting clear, achievable goals can help you stay focused and motivated. Whether it's completing a project, learning a new framework, or passing a certification exam, having specific goals will give you something to work towards.

- Celebrate Achievements: Take time to celebrate your achievements, no matter how small. Completing a project, solving a tricky bug, or learning a new concept are all milestones worth celebrating. Recognizing your progress will boost your confidence and keep you motivated.

- Stay Curious: Cultivate a mindset of curiosity and exploration. The world of programming is vast, and there's always something new to learn. Stay curious, ask questions, and never stop exploring new topics and technologies.

- Take Breaks: Don't forget to take breaks and give yourself time to rest. Taking a break can help clear your mind, reduce stress, and improve your overall productivity. Remember, it's a marathon, not a sprint.

Embrace the Journey

Programming is a lifelong journey of learning and discovery. There will always be new challenges, new technologies, and new opportunities to grow. Embrace the journey, and don't be afraid to make mistakes along the way. Every mistake is a learning opportunity, and every challenge is a chance to improve.

You've come a long way, and you've built a strong foundation in Java programming. With dedication, curiosity, and a willingness to keep learning, there's no limit to what you can achieve. Whether you become a professional software developer, build your own projects, or simply enjoy coding as a hobby, the skills you've gained will serve you well.

Thank you for joining me on this journey through Java programming. I'm excited to see where your path takes you next. Happy Coding!